Tatsuki Fujimoto

I love *Sadoko vs. Kayako*!

Tatsuki Fujimoto won Honorable Mention in the November 2013 Shueisha Crown Newcomers' Awards for his debut one-shot story *Love Is Blind*. His first series, *Fire Punch*, ran for eight volumes. Chainsaw Man began serialization in 2018 in *Weekly Shonen Jump*.

4

SHONEN JUMP Manga Edition

Story & Art **TATSUKI FUJIMOTO**

Translation/AMANDA HALEY
Touch-Up Art & Lettering/JAMES GAUBATZ
Design/JULIAN [JR] ROBINSON
Editor/ALEXIS KIRSCH

CHAINSAW MAN © 2018 by Tatsuki Fujimoto
All rights reserved.

First published in Japan in 2018 by SHUEISHA Inc., Tokyo.
English translation rights arranged by SHUEISHA Inc.

The stories, characters and incidents mentioned in this publication are entirely fictional.

No portion of this book may be reproduced or transmitted in any form or by any means without written permission from the copyright holders.

Printed in the U.S.A.

Published by VIZ Media, LLC
P.O. Box 77010
San Francisco, CA 94107

10 9 8
First printing, April 2021
Eighth printing, April 2022

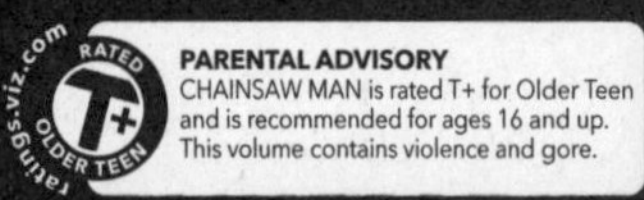

CHAINSAW MAN

4

The Gun is Mightier

Tatsuki Fujimoto

CHARACTERS

Denji

A young man-slash-Chainsaw Devil who carries his partner Pochita inside him. He's always true to his desires. Likes Makima, the first person to ever treat him like a human being.

Pochita

Chainsaw Devil. Gave up his heart to Denji, becoming part of his body.

Makima

The mysterious woman in charge of Public Safety Devil Extermination Special Division 4. Can smell devil scents.

Aki Hayakawa

Makima's loyal subordinate. Denji's senior at Public Safety by three years, he's assigned to keep an eye on him.

Himeno

Hayakawa's work senior and paired with him as his buddy. Contracted with the Ghost Devil.

Power

Blood Devil Fiend. Egotistical and prone to going out of control. Her cat Meowy is her only friend.

Hirokazu Arai

Himeno's uptight, hot-blooded subordinate. Doesn't trust Denji and Power.

Kobeni Higashiyama

A timid new recruit. Though mentally frail, her boss Himeno thinks she has talent.

Samurai Sword

Grandson of the yakuza who drove Denji into a debt trap. Won't stay dead…?

Hoodie Girl

Working with Samurai Sword. Uses a powerful devil that looks like a snake.

STORY

Denji is a young man who hunts devils with his pet devil-dog Pochita. To pay off his debts, Denji is forced to live in extreme poverty and worked like a dog, only to be betrayed and killed on the job without ever getting to live a decent life. But Pochita, at the cost of the pooch's own life, brings Denji back—as Chainsaw Man! After Denji buzzes through all their attackers, he's taken in by the mysterious Makima and begins a new life as a Public Safety Devil Hunter.

After the fight against the Eternity Devil, Hayakawa and Himeno grow suspicious of the secrets surrounding Denji, but Makima won't let anything slip. Denji himself is hyped for his French kiss reward from Himeno…until it changes into an unwanted barf kiss.

The next week, Makima is attacked by a group using guns. The emergency quickly escalates as Special Division 4 members are gunned down one after another! Denji's team is ambushed by a mysterious swordsman and girl who are after Denji's heart at the Gun Devil's request. Aki uses the Curse Devil's power against the strong pair, but it fails. Worse still, Himeno offers all of herself to the Ghost Devil and disappears to save Aki. The stakes couldn't be higher as Denji turns into Chainsaw Man and confronts these new enemies!

CONTENTS

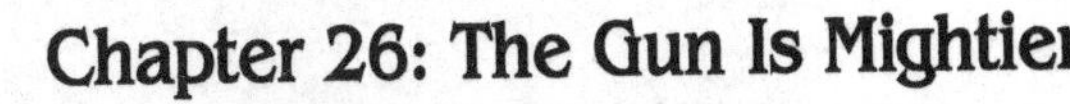
Chapter 26: The Gun Is Mightier

THIS IS SAWATARI.
WE'RE ENGAGED IN COMBAT WITH CHAINSAW ON THE THIRD FLOOR OF THE NERIMA NISHIDAI BUILDING.
BRING BACK-UP.

BRM
BRM

BRM
BRM
BRM

BZZZ
KR

RAAH!!
SMASH

OW!!

DASH
VMM

DO WE SHOOT, SIR?
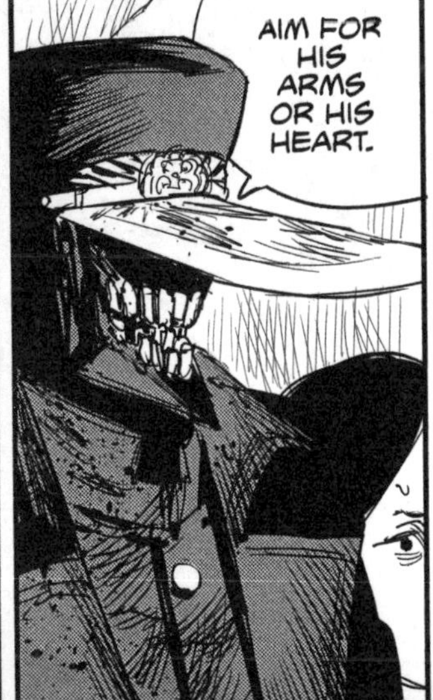
AIM FOR HIS ARMS OR HIS HEART.

TAKE ...
BAM
WHAM

...THIS!

IIING
OW?!
THAT REALLY HURTS!
WHUUUH?! WHEN DID I GET CUT?!
BANG
YOW!!
BANG
OUCH!!
BANG

HRAH!

HEY! BAD GUY!!
UNGH!
THIS GUY'S YOUR BUDDY, RIGHT?!

AND IF HE IS? THEN WHAT?

If you move even one millimeter...
...buddy boy's face here is gonna be mincemeat!!

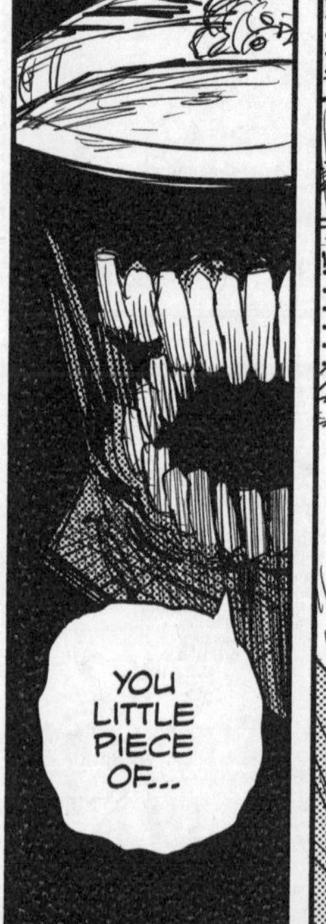
YOU LITTLE PIECE OF...

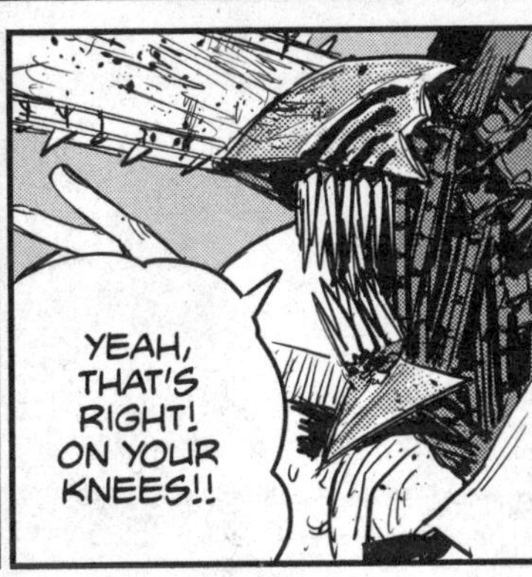
YEAH, THAT'S RIGHT! ON YOUR KNEES!!

HUH?
HE DISAP-PEARED?!

AH!

UUUGH ...

I'LL CARRY HIM.
YOU GO GET THE CAR.

HURRY UP!
THOUGH CHAINSAW'S FRIENDS SHOULD ALL BE SHOT DEAD BY NOW...

GUH ...!
SPLIK
SPLAT

EVEN DEVIL HUNTERS ARE ONLY HUMAN!
THEY CAN'T WIN AGAINST GUNS!

THEY HAVE GUNS!
AHHH! AH...!

WE'RE ALMOST AT THE STATION.
MOVE TO ANOTHER TRAIN CAR AND BLEND IN WITH THE CIVILIANS.

WHAT
THE
—?!

京都駅
Kyōto

WE'VE RECEIVED WORD THAT SPECIAL DIVISIONS 1, 2, 3 AND 4 WERE ALL AMBUSHED WITH GUNS IN TOKYO...
WHAT ?!

FOR REAL...? MAKIMA'S DEAD?
SO WE WAITED HERE FOR NOTHING?!

KUROSE.

TENDO.

WE CAME UNDER GUNFIRE ON THE SHINKAN-SEN.
THERE ARE BODIES IN THERE. HAVE THEM CLEANED UP.
THE LUNCHEON IS CANCELED.

THERE WAS GUN-FIRE IN TOKYO TOO—
MISS MAKIMA, THAT BLOOD!!
WERE YOU SHOT?!
IT'S NOT MINE.

Chain sa w man

Chapter 27: From Kyoto

THE ENEMY'S TARGET IS PROBABLY DENJI.

WE'LL DEAL WITH IT RIGHT HERE.

KUROSE.

GO BORROW ABOUT 30 CONVICTS SERVING LIFE SENTENCES OR WORSE FROM THE MINISTRY OF JUSTICE.

TENDO.

RENT OUT A NEARBY SHRINE. ONE AT THE HIGHEST ALTITUDE POSSIBLE.

ALSO, SOMEONE GET ME A CHANGE OF CLOTHES.

カメレオン

HURRY!

I WON'T BE ABLE TO FIGHT FOR A WHILE NOW, YOU KNOW.

MM.

GRAB THAT SIDE!
BLECH!
WHERE AM I SUPPOSED TO HOLD...?

やきとり
バンバン看板店

Come on! Grab it!

Hey!

カラオケ
くすり
I JUST...
WHAT THE HELL...?

Don't start freaking out!
Grab it!

LISTEN! SOMETHING FEELS WRONG!!

HUH ?!

WHAT DO YOU MEA—

WH—
HOLY ----!!

TEAM E!
HAVE TEAM C RECONFIRM MAKIMA'S DEATH!

THIS IS TEAM E.
THIS IS TEAM E.

WE'VE BEEN UNABLE TO MAKE CONTACT WITH TEAM C FOR—
AAAH!!

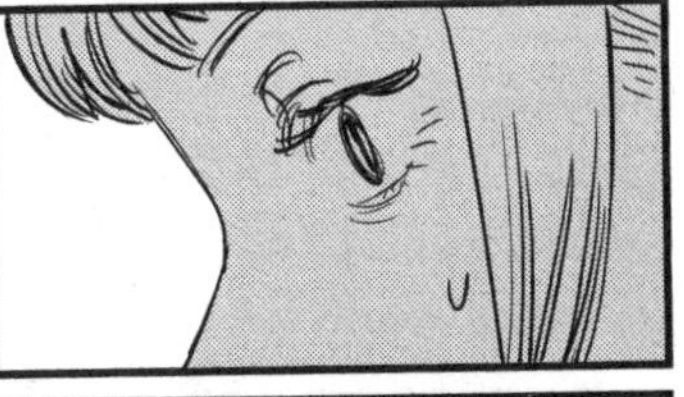

THAT WOMAN ...

WHY DO WE NEED BLIND-FOLDS TOO...?

MAKIMA REPORTS DIRECTLY TO THE CHIEF CABINET SECRETARY.
ORDINARY DEVIL HUNTERS AREN'T AUTHORIZED TO KNOW WHICH DEVILS SHE HAS CONTRACTS WITH.

SAY...
..."SHUZO MISHIMA."
SHUZO MISHIMA...

FF
PA

HEY! PUT HIM IN THE VAN!

HEY! DO YOU HEAR ME?!

MISHIMA!!

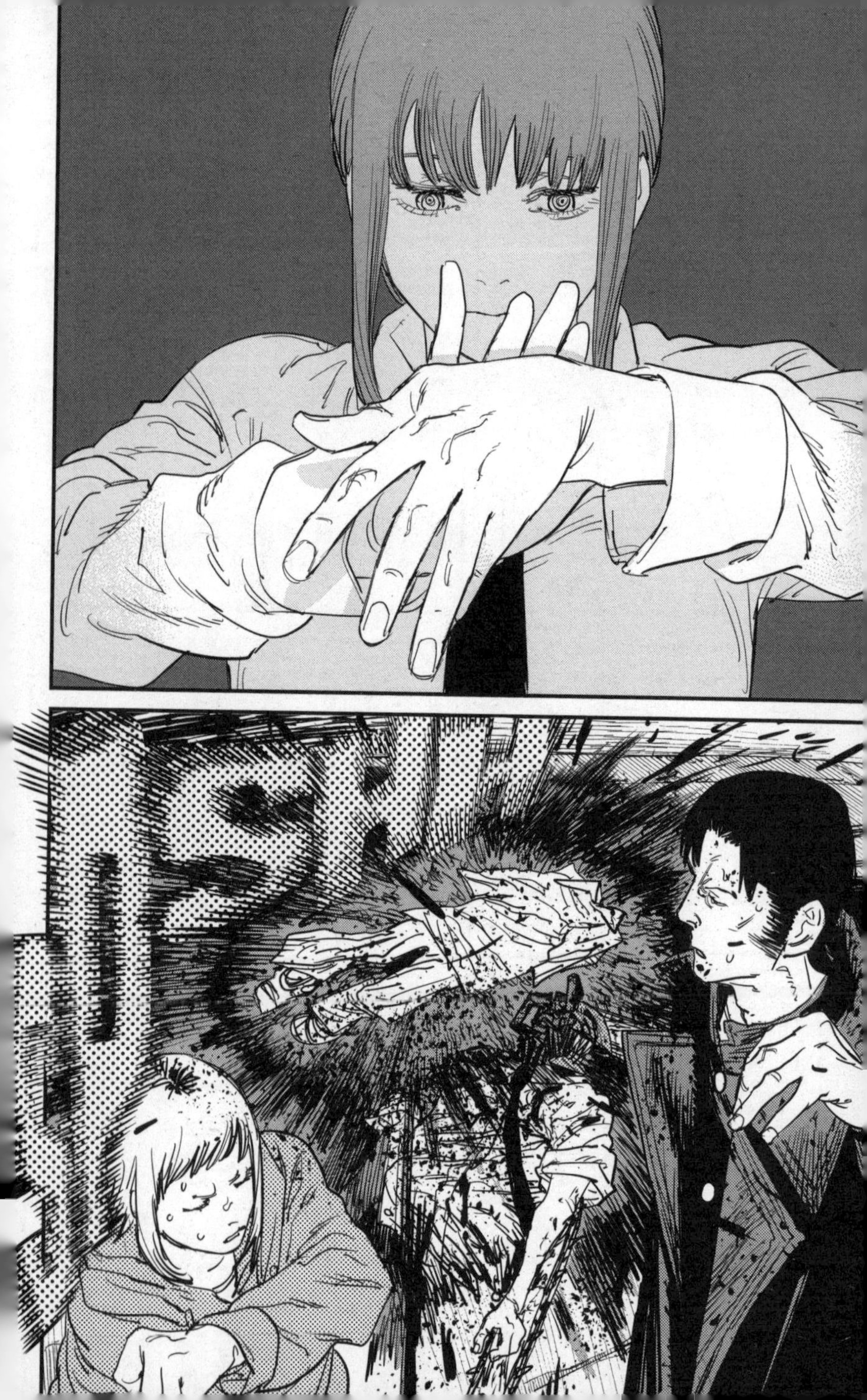

ZSH

SAY, "TAKASHI INOUE."

TAKASHI INOUE...?

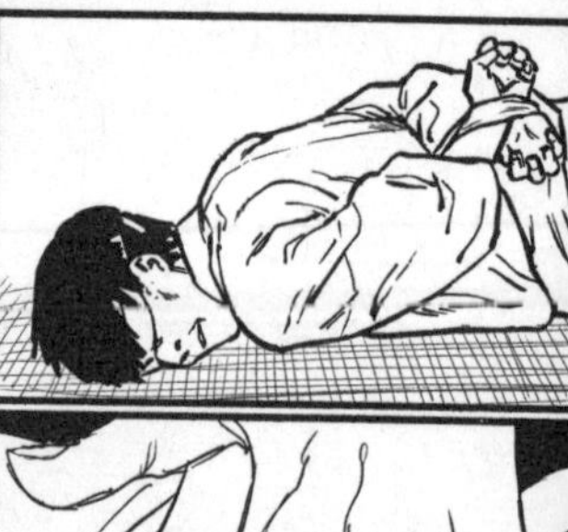

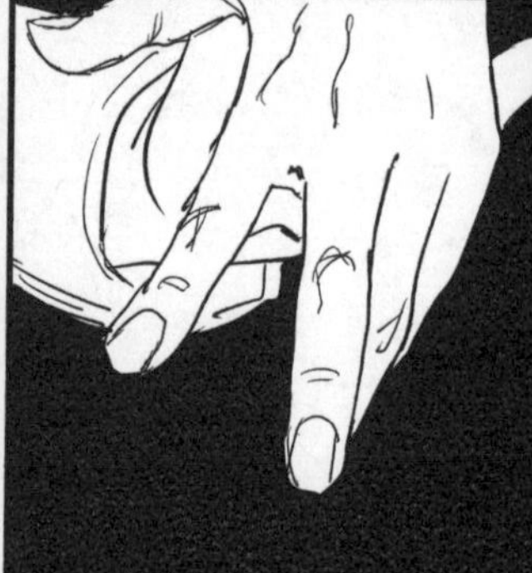

HEY! HEY!!
SOME-BODY HELP ME!!

IT STOPPED ...?

YOU CAN REMOVE THOSE NOW.

I'VE FINISHED WHAT I CAN DO FROM HERE.

I'M RETURNING TO TOKYO.

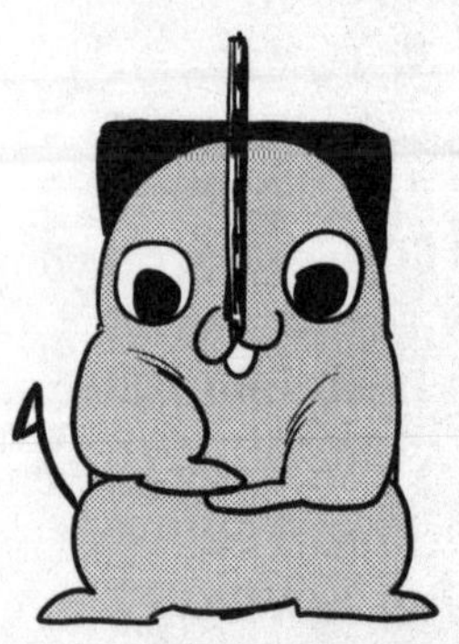

Chain saw man

Chapter 28: Secrets & Lies

BANG

SWSH

BANG

YOU PEOPLE ARE THE SHOOTERS, RIGHT?

BWOO
OO

TP TP TP TP TP
WHAT IS SHE, A MONKEY?!

KLIK
KL
IK

WR

CHING

BANG
BANG

DIE
INSIDE
THE VAN!

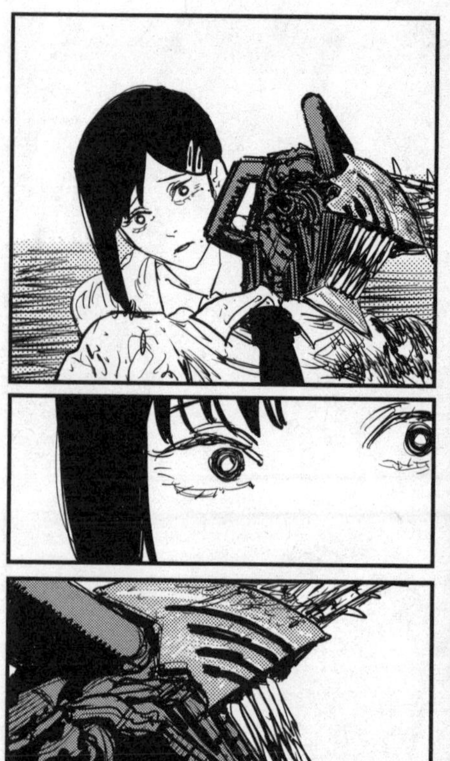

SORRY I TRIED TO KILL YOU BEFORE ...

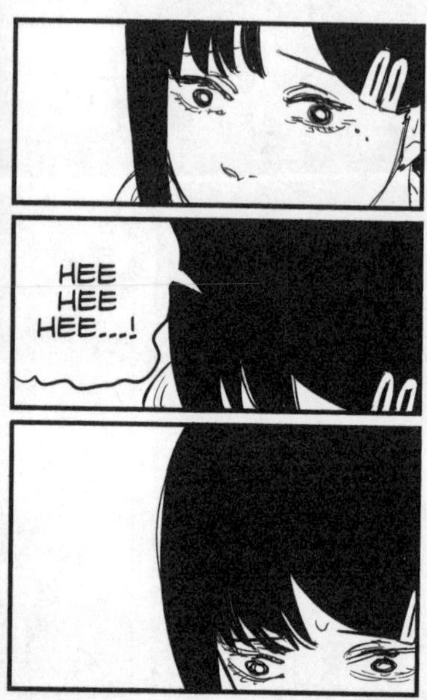
HEE
HEE
HEE...!

"SORRY I TRIED TO KILL YOU"...?!
THAT'S HILARIOUS!
HEE HEE HEE HEE HEE HEE HEE HEE...!

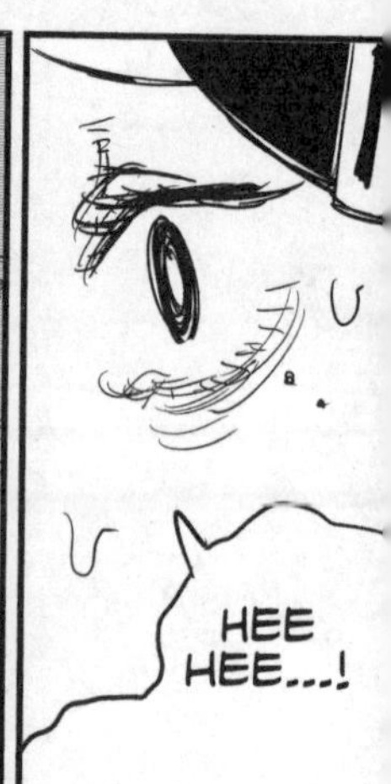
HEE HEE...!
I CAN'T... IT'S LIKE I'M *HIGH*...

HE SHIELDED ME... *ME*...
FOR ME, HE...!
ME... HEE HEE HEE...!

I CAN'T TAKE IT ANYMORE...
THIS JOB IS GOING TO DRIVE ME CRAZY...

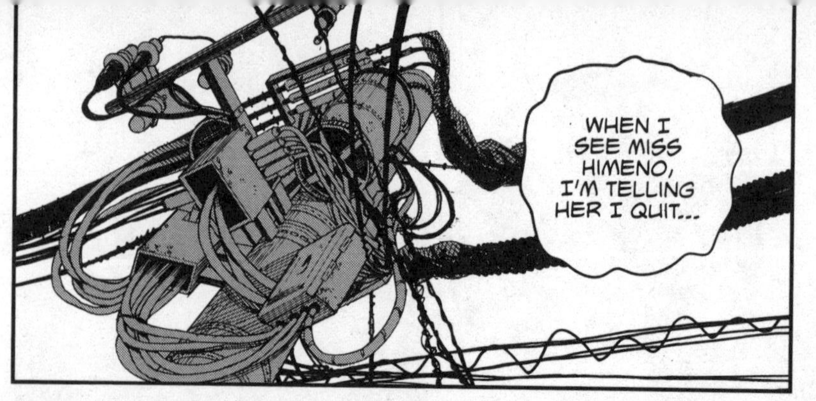

東京駅
TōKyō

MADOKA. GLAD YOU'RE ALIVE.
HOW MUCH OF THE SPECIAL DIVISION SURVIVED?

SPECIAL DIVISIONS 1, 2, 3 AND 4 CAME UNDER GUNFIRE SIMULTANE-OUSLY.
ASIDE FROM THE NON-HUMANS, ALMOST EVERYONE DIED.

A SHOOTING SPECIFICALLY TARGETING THE SPECIAL DIVISION...
ODDS ARE THE GUN DEVIL IS INVOLVED.

I HAVE A MESSAGE FROM THE HIGHER-UPS.
DUE TO THE PERSONNEL SHORTAGE, SPECIAL DIVISIONS 1, 2 AND 3 WILL MERGE WITH SPECIAL DIVISION 4.
FROM THIS POINT FORWARD, THEY'RE PLACING PUBLIC SAFETY DEVIL EXTERMINATION SPECIAL DIVISION 4 UNDER YOUR COMMAND.

ALSO, THIS IS FOR YOU.
WHAT IS IT?

MY RESIG-NATION.

YOU'RE QUITTING?
THE SPECIAL DIVISION'S GOTTEN SINISTER.
IT'S QUIT OR BE KILLED.

I SEE...

ANSWER ONE LAST QUESTION FOR ME.
HOW MUCH OF THIS HAD YOU ANTICIPATED?

I'M REALLY NOT AT LIBERTY TO DISCUSS PUBLIC SAFETY'S INTERNAL AFFAIRS WITH CIVILIANS.

THANK YOU FOR YOUR SERVICE, MADOKA.
I'LL PASS THIS ON.

UH... MISS MAKIMA? YOU KNOW IT'S NOT LIKE WE'RE JOINING YOUR SPECIAL DIVISION, RIGHT...?

WE'RE ONLY HERE FOR TRAINING, YOU KNOW...?
ONE WEEK FROM NOW, WE'LL BE ON OUR WAY BACK TO KYOTO...

THAT'S A SHAME.
THERE ARE SO MANY GREAT RESTAURANTS IN TOKYO...

Chainsaw man

Chapter 29: Perfect Score

7:10

Public Safety Devil Hunters Engage in Large-Scale Combat in Nerima

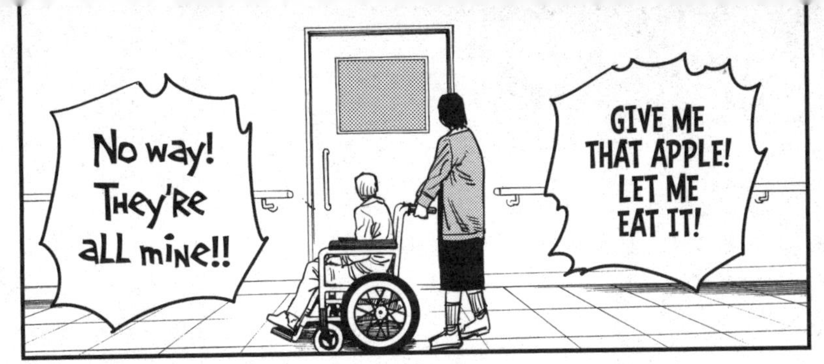
GIVE ME THAT APPLE! LET ME EAT IT!
No way! They're all mine!!

No apples for jerks who ran away from the enemy!!

I NEVER FLED!!
I LEFT BECAUSE I WAS HUNGRY, THAT'S ALL!!

Liar!! Scaredy-cat! Chicken!
WHY, YOU!

WHO ELSE FROM DIVISION 4 IS STILL ALIVE...?

THAT SHORTY CALLED KOBENI ...

I GUESS THE GUY WITH THE GLASSES SURVIVED TOO. 'CEPT HE QUIT PUBLIC SAFETY.

I'LL LEAVE YOU ONE CUZ I'M NICE.
SEE YA.

KLAK

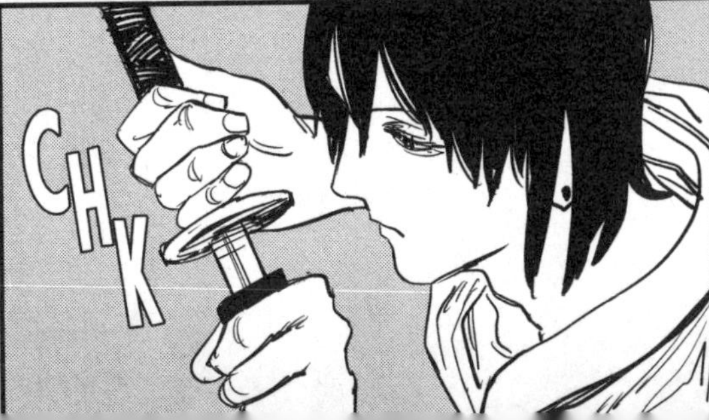
CHK

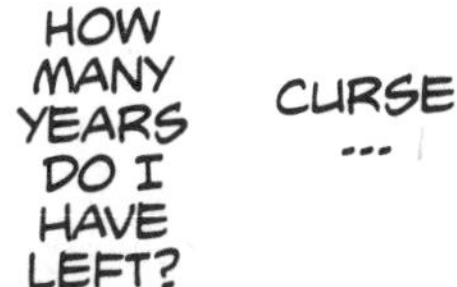
CURSE ...
HOW MANY YEARS DO I HAVE LEFT?

TWO YEARS ...
FLIK
FLIK
FLIK

UHHN...
GHK...
CAME BACK CUZ I LEFT MY MANGA, AND HE'S CRYING... AWKWARD...
WELL, YEAH, OF COURSE HE'S CRYING!
A BUNCH OF HIS WORK PALS BIT IT, I GUESS...
...AND HIS BUDDY HIMENO IS DEAD TOO. MAKES SENSE.

WAIT A SEC...

HUUUUH?

I'VE GOT...

... NOTHIN'.

I CAN'T, LIKE, CRY AT ALL...

HMM... I WAS SAD WHEN POCHITA DIED.

BUT HIMENO'S DEATH... NOT REALLY...?

SHE WAS THE FIRST PERSON TO EVER SAY SHE'D BE MY FRIEND TOO...
AM I, LIKE... A HEARTLESS JERK?

WOULD I CRY IF POWER DIED?

NAAAH... DON'T THINK SO.

WHAT IF THAT JERK DIED?

THAT'S A NOPE.

WHAT IF MAKIMA DIED...?

IF MAKIMA DIED...
...I'D PROBABLY BE DOWN IN THE DUMPS FOR A WHILE...
...BUT I THINK I'D BE BACK TO HAPPY IN THREE DAYS.
CUZ...FOR ME, AS LONG AS I GOT THREE SQUARE MEALS A DAY, A GOOD NIGHT'S SLEEP AND A BATH, I'M LIVING THE HIGH LIFE...

Eh, what-ever! Forget the serious stuff!

UNHAPPY THOUGHTS WILL ONLY MAKE YOU UNHAPPY!

C'MON, LET'S GO SEE MAKIMA!
UGH, HOW DEPRESS-ING!

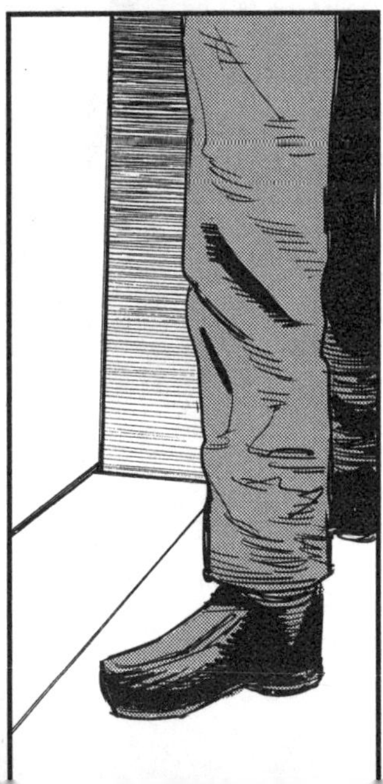

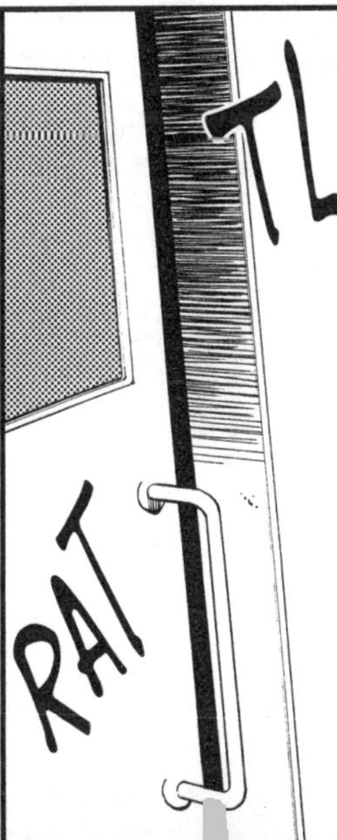
RATTL

EX-
CUSE
US.
HELLO.

WHAT'S THIS NOW? WERE YOU CRYING?
SHOULD WE STEP OUT?

WHO ARE YOU...?

WE'RE FROM KYOTO. WE'RE HERE TO TRAIN SPECIAL DIVISION 4 AT MAKIMA'S REQUEST.
CAN I EAT THAT APPLE?

TRAIN US...?

THE HOTEL INCIDENT AND THIS LATEST ATTACK PROVED THAT THE ENEMY FORCES ARE TARGETING YOU, DENJI.
I WAS PLANNING TO STRENGTHEN DIVISION 4, BUT THEN MOST OF YOU WENT AND DIED.

THIS IS—
SHHH!
QUIET.

ANSWER MY QUESTIONS.

WHAT DID YOU FEEL WHEN YOUR TEAMMATES DIED?

NOTHIN' MUCH?
I WAS LIKE, "THEY'RE DEAD!"

DO YOU WANT TO GET REVENGE?

I DON'T LIKE REVENGE STUFF. TOO DARK AND BROODING.
ME TOO!

HUMANS OR DEVILS—WHICH SIDE ARE YOU ON?

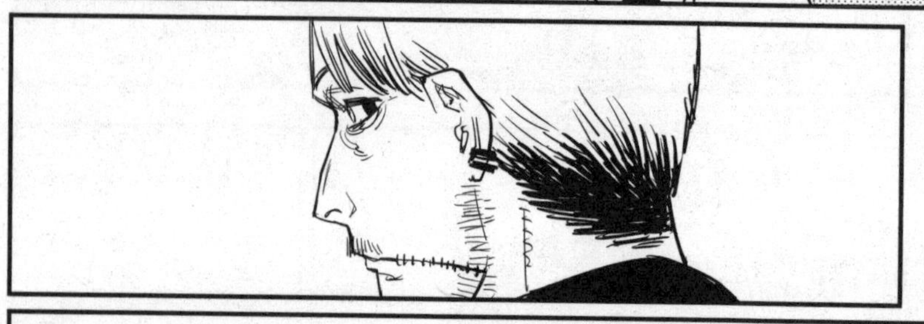

YOU BOTH GET A PERFECT SCORE.

TYPES LIKE YOU TWO ARE FEW AND FAR BETWEEN.
EXCEL-LENT.

HUH?

I LOVE YA.

MAKIMA, YOU CAN GO.
THEIR TRAINING BEGINS RIGHT HERE AND NOW.

I'M SCARED.

WELL, I'LL LEAVE YOU TO IT.
MISS MAKIMA?!
SWFF

HUH?

HUH?

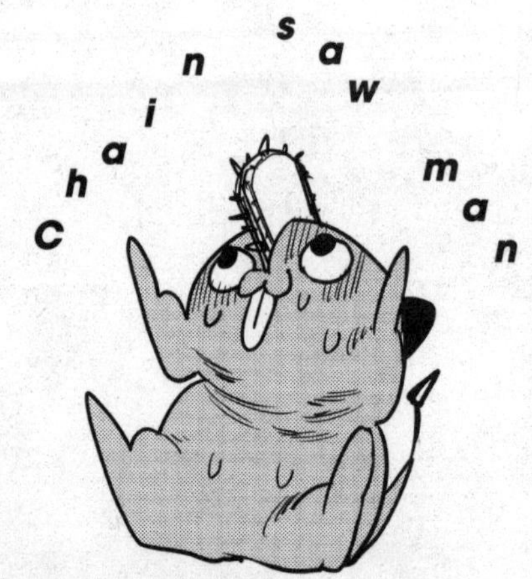
Chainsawman

Chapter 30: Bruised & Battered

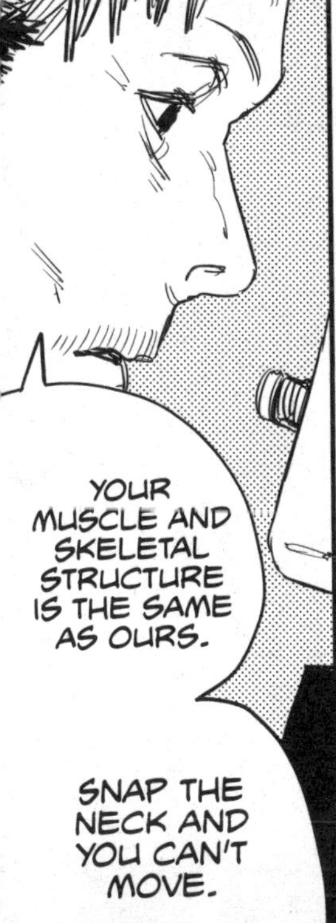

THE DIFFERENCE BETWEEN YOU AND HUMANS IS...

I SMELL BLOOD!!

MAKIMA ASKED ME TO TRAIN YOU KIDDOS UP.

SHE MUST BE IN A FIX, SINCE THE GUN DEVIL'S AFTER YOUR HEART FOR WHATEVER REASON...
...BUT YOU'RE JUST A SMALL FRY WHO CAN BE CRUSHED IN NO TIME FLAT.

WHY DID YOU JUST ATTACK US?!

I'VE TRAINED HUMANS BEFORE, BUT DEVILS LIKE YOU TWO? NEVER DONE IT, NOT ONCE.
I THOUGHT ABOUT WHAT TO DO WHILE I WAS DRUNK.
AND THEN A LIGHT BULB FINALLY WENT OFF IN MY ALCOHOL-ADDLED BRAIN.

I'M THE STRONGEST DEVIL HUNTER.

A DEVIL WHO CAN TAKE DOWN A POWERHOUSE LIKE ME WOULD BE A POWERHOUSE THEMSELVES...

SO I'M GONNA KEEP HUNTIN' YOU TWO...

...UNTIL YOU'RE ABLE TO DEFEAT ME.

HE'S OUT OF HIS MIND!

TOTALLY!

LET'S TRY THIS AGAIN.

DRUNK GEEZER OR NO, WE'LL GET ARRESTED IF WE GO AND KILL HIM!

SPLURT

DENJI!
PAFF

SHIK SHIK
SHIK
SHIK
SHNK

THE BOY'S IMMORTAL. THE FIEND'S SEMI-IMMORTAL.

AND YOU HAVE THE MINDSET TO BE ABLE TO BASH A PERSON'S HEAD IN WITH NO HESITATION.

NEITHER OF YOU HAS HUMAN RIGHTS.

EVER SINCE I WAS A TYKE, I'VE BEEN SO STRONG THAT I'D BREAK MY TOYS IN NO TIME.

I ALWAYS WANTED SOME UNBREAKABLE TOYS...

I'LL TURN YOU INTO THE BADDEST OF THE BADASSES.

SEE? IT WON'T COME, RIGHT?

YOU USED THE FOX RECKLESSLY AND GOT ON ITS BAD SIDE.
IT PROBABLY WON'T EVER LET YOU USE IT AGAIN.

AND THAT SWORD IS FROM THE CURSE DEVIL, RIGHT?
HOW MANY MORE TIMES CAN YOU USE THAT?

SO THAT'S WHAT YOU MEANT BY "TRAINING."

GLAD YOU'RE SO QUICK ON THE UPTAKE.

WE'RE HERE TO DO CAREER COACHING FOR THE HUMANS IN THE SPECIAL DIVISION.

THIS MAY BE INAPPROPRIATE TO SAY, BUT WE EXPECTED YOU TO CALL IT QUITS AFTER THIS LATEST INCIDENT.

AND IN FACT, SOMEONE FROM YOUR DIVISION DID MOVE TO THE CIVILIAN SECTOR.

WILL YOU QUIT PUBLIC SAFETY AND ENJOY THE LIFE YOU HAVE LEFT?

OR WILL YOU STAY ON AND SEE HELL?

HOW COULD I QUIT...?

I SEE...
UNDER-STOOD.

IT'S ALREADY PRETTY LATE. WE'LL LEAVE FOR TODAY.
WE'LL BE BACK TOMORROW WITH THE PAPERWORK AND WHATNOT.

LOOKS LIKE WHAT OUR SENIOR IN KYOTO TOLD US WAS TRUE.

"BE CAREFUL— EVERYBODY IN THE SPECIAL DIVISIONS IS INSANE"...

...THEY SAID.

TAKE YOUR TIME.

RATTL

I'M GOIN' HOME TO SLEEP.
I'LL PICK YOU UP AT YOUR PLACE TOMOR-ROW.

WAAH...
WAAH
...

THUD

THUMP
THUMP
THUMP
HIS BRAIN BROKE AGAIN!
GET BETTER! GET BETTER!

GASP...!
OAUGH...
HOW MANY TIMES DID I GET KILLED TODAY?!

AT LEAST 20!
I'M NOT EXACTLY SURE BECAUSE WHENEVER YOU DIED, I WAS USUALLY UNCONSCIOUS TOO.

IF WE GOTTA KEEP LIVIN' LIKE THIS, WE'RE GONNA BE SERIOUSLY UNHAPPY.
THAT GEEZER'S TOO STRONG...

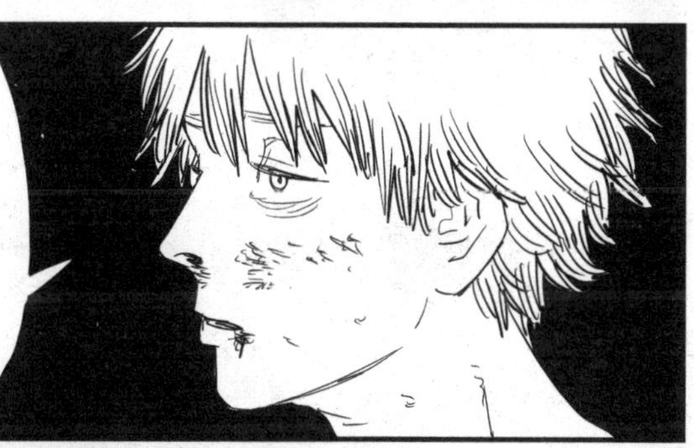
I WORKED HARD SO FAR TO GET HAPPINESS. NOW IT'S WORK HARD AND BE UNHAPPY? THAT'S CRAP.

SHOULD WE FLEE TOGETHER?

IF WE RAN, IT'D BE RUNNING FROM PUBLIC SAFETY. PRETTY SURE THIS TIME WE'D GET THE DEVIL TREATMENT FOR REAL.

HE'S SUPER STRONG! *BUT!*

ALCOHOL HAS ROTTED HIS BRAIN!

WE SHOULD FIGHT HIM USING OUR MINDS!!

I SEE, I SEE!

YEAH, I'VE BEEN TOTALLY THINKING ABOUT THAT LATELY TOO!

LIKE, HOW COOL WOULD IT BE IF I COULD FIGHT LIKE ONE OF THOSE BRAINY CHARACTERS IN MANGA AND STUFF?!

LET'S MURDER HIM WITH OUR INTELLECT!!

OH MAN! I FEEL LIKE I'VE GOTTEN WAY SMARTER ALREADY!!

Chain
saw man

DAMN PUNKS DITCHED MY TRAINING...

Chapter 31: The Future Rules

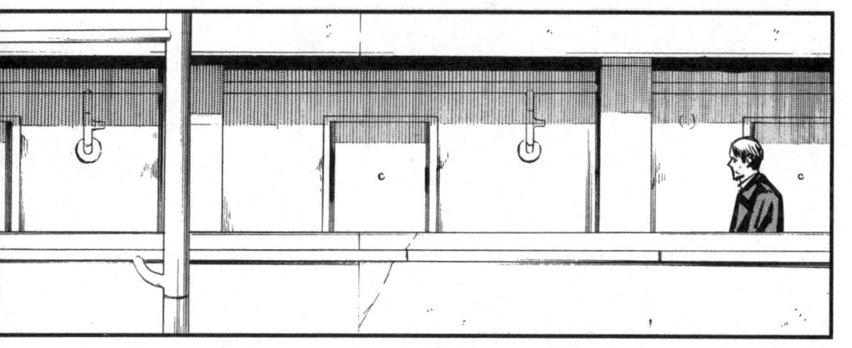

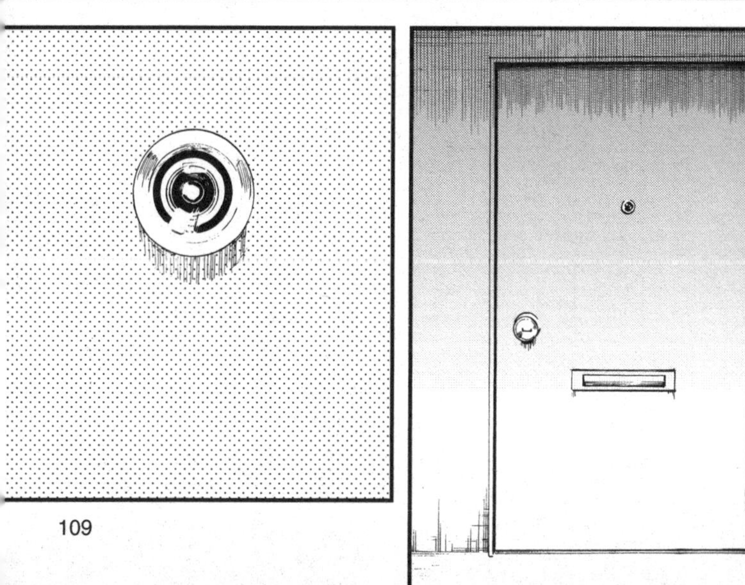

THE SCENT OF THIS BLOOD ...
IT'S THE DRUNK GEEZER. HE'S HERE.
ANYBODY WHO RUINS OUR DAILY LIFE...
...HAS GOTTA DIE.

COMMENCE OPERATION: SUPER-SMART!

THRUNK

WHOA!

SO THE HUNTER IS NOW THE HUNTED.
SN
AP

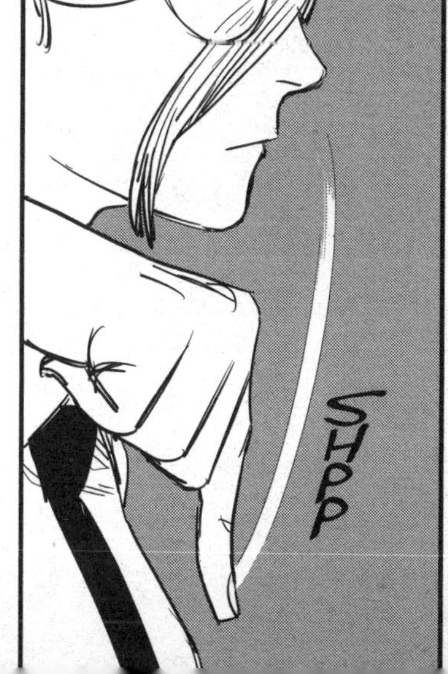
SHPP

KRAK
THWAK

F
PP
SMACK

BWOOSH
WHAM

THAT WAS YOUR BEST TRY YET.
OWWWW...
SO CORNERED PREY WILL USE THEIR BRAINS.
USE YOUR HEADS EVEN MORE.

THERE ARE TWO REASONS YOU LOST THIS TIME.

ONE, POWER USES TOO MUCH BLOOD FIGHTING LIKE THAT. HER ACTUAL BODY ENDS UP ANEMIC.
TWO, DENJI, YOU COULDN'T PREDICT MY ATTACK.

YOU DID GOOD THIS TIME. WE'RE DONE FOR THE DAY.
I'M GOING DRINK-ING.
POWY... HE SAID WE'RE DONE FOR THE DAY...
LUCKY US...

THUNK

WH...
WHUUH
...?

HAVING YOU CONTRACT WITH A STRONGER DEVIL MEANS THE SPECIFICS OF THE CONTRACT WILL PROBABLY BE PRETTY BRUTAL.

BUT WE WOULDN'T DO THAT OUT OF CRUELTY, YOU KNOW.

102
THIS IS WHERE DEVILS CAPTURED ALIVE BY PUBLIC SAFETY ARE LOCKED UP.
LET'S FIND YOU A WEAPON IN HERE.

ON AN UNRELATED NOTE, THAT BEAUTY FROM YESTERDAY...
SHE YOUR GIRL-FRIEND?

GET YOUR MIND OUT OF THE GUTTER.

THAT WAS MY BUDDY'S YOUNGER SISTER.
UH-OH... DID SHE HIT YOU?
NO...
SHE GAVE ME LETTERS.

LETTERS?

THESE ARE THE LETTERS MY SISTER SENT ME.
YOU SHOULD READ THEM, SO I'M PASSING THEM ON TO YOU.

Is Dad feeling better?

allowance

m not hurting for food or anything.

'ou don't have to send me rice anymore.

but if you

How's Dad doing lately? Are you
making sure he takes his medicine?
I think you could

I made Aki get some piercings.
He was really annoyed.

I don't think I can do it after all.

How can I get Aki to quit? He'll just brush me off with some non-answer aga

IN HERE IS THE *FUTURE DEVIL.*

TWO PEOPLE IN PUBLIC SAFETY HAVE A CONTRACT WITH THIS ONE.

ONE OF THEM GAVE HALF THEIR LIFE SPAN.

THE OTHER GAVE IT BOTH EYES, THEIR SENSE OF TASTE AND THEIR SENSE OF SMELL.

SLAM

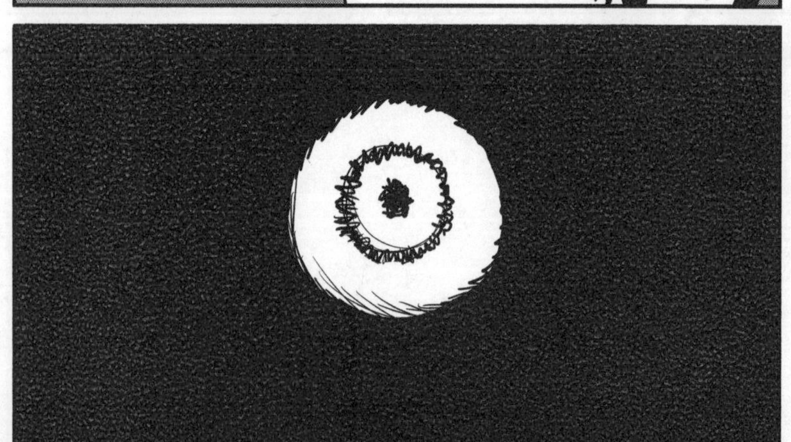

THE FUTURE ...
... RULES.
THE FUTURE!
RULES!
THE FUTURE !!
RULES !!

Chain
saw man

Chapter 32: Over and Over Again

I COME UP WITH THE DETAILS OF A CONTRACT DEPENDING ON THE FUTURE!
BUT WHATEVER. SHOW ME YOUR FUTURE!

HURRY UP AND STICK YOUR FACE IN MY BELLY!
HOW ELSE AM I GONNA SEE YOUR FUTURE?!

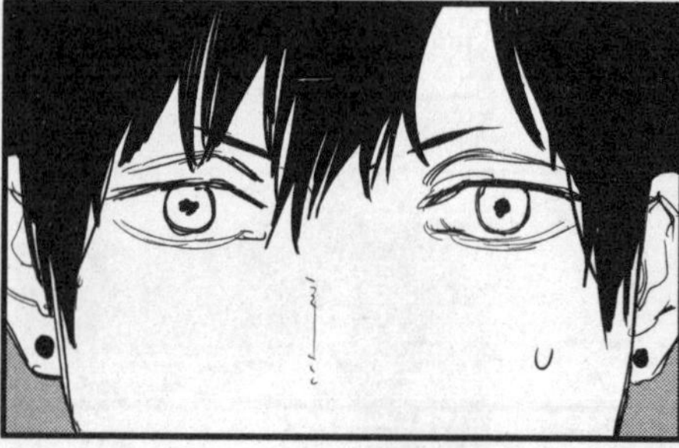

MM?

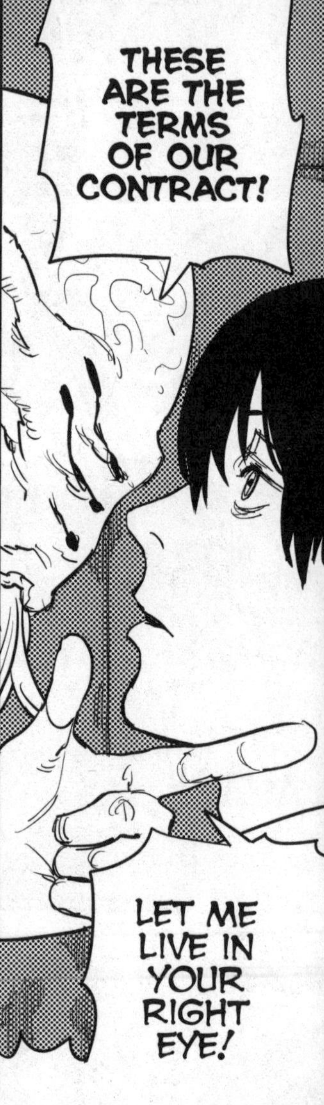
THESE ARE THE TERMS OF OUR CONTRACT!
LET ME LIVE IN YOUR RIGHT EYE!
DO THAT, AND I'LL HELP YOU!

YOU LOOK LIKE YOU'RE THINKING, "THAT'S IT?"

I FEEL LIKE SEEING YOUR FUTURE WITH MY OWN EYES.

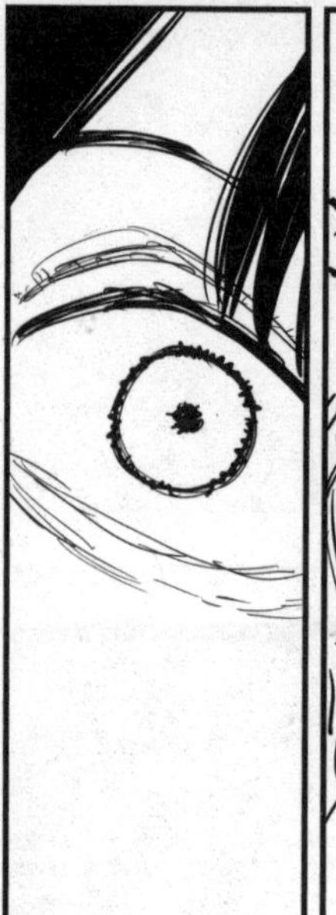

BECAUSE IN THE FUTURE, YOU'RE GOING TO DIE IN THE WORST POSSIBLE WAY!

DON'T BOTHER.

I'M NOT INTERESTED IN HOW *I'LL* DIE.

AS LONG AS I CAN KILL THOSE I WANT TO KILL...

...I DON'T CARE WHAT COMES AFTER.

NOW GET IN MY EYE.

MM...
ALL RIGHT.

YOUR MOVES JUST NOW GET A PERFECT SCORE.
FROM NOW ON, YOUR TRAINING DOESN'T NEED TO BE DAILY.
WE'LL DO IT ONCE A WEEK.

KEEP A COOL HEAD, EVEN WHEN YOU HAVE A BATTLE HIGH.
ALWAYS KEEP YOUR WEAPONS AND THE SITUATION IN MIND.
YAAA... Y...
HOORAY ...!

IN LIGHT OF YOUR TRAINING, YOU'RE READY FOR REAL COMBAT TOMORROW.
REAL COMBAT ?

WE'RE HEADING OUT TO CAPTURE THE ONES WHO KILLED HIMENO AND THE REST—SAMURAI SWORD AND SNAKE GIRL.
IT'LL BE THE NEW DIVISION 4'S DEBUT.

IF THE MISSION FAILS, DIVISION 4 IS DONE.
AND IF THAT HAPPENS, YOU TWO WILL BE PUT DOWN VIA A REAL BATTLE WITH ME.

IF THAT HAPPENS, I'LL LETCHA GO WITHOUT KILLING YOU.

HUH?

CUZ YOU MADE ME STRONGER.
NOW I CAN KILL MORE DEVILS.

And if I do THAT, I GOT a date WITH Makima!!

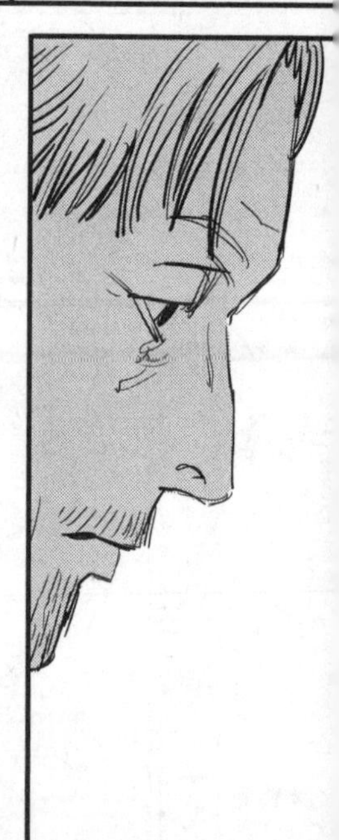

GOOD WORK. I KNOW YOU'VE BEEN QUITE BUSY.
I'M COUNTING ON YOU TO KEEP TRAINING DENJI AND POWER.

I'VE GOTTEN SICK OF 'EM ALREADY.

EVERY TIME A DOG I TRAINED DIES, I DRINK MORE AND MORE.
I THOUGHT WITH *TOYS* I'D FEEL NO GUILT, EVEN IF THEY BROKE...

BUT MY MIND'S GOTTEN WEAK WITH AGE. EVEN TOYS HAVE ME FEELING THINGS.

SO...
WHAT DID YOU WANT TO TALK ABOUT?

THE AMBUSH ON THE SPECIAL DIVISIONS... PUBLIC SAFETY ARE NO FOOLS.
YOU KNEW ABOUT IT AND LET IT HAPPEN, DIDN'T YOU?

I CAME UNDER GUNFIRE MYSELF, YOU KNOW.

WHATEVER INHUMAN DEEDS YOU DO...
...EVEN IF YOU KILL MY PET DOGS...

...AS LONG AS YOU'RE ON HUMANITY'S SIDE, I'LL LOOK THE OTHER WAY.

ONLY AS LONG AS THAT'S TRUE.

ALL I WANT IS TO SAVE AS MANY PEOPLE FROM THE DEVILS AS POSSIBLE.

IT'S BEEN DECIDED THAT IF THIS MISSION SUCCEEDS, THE EXISTENCE OF DIVISION 4 WILL BE AGGRESSIVELY REPORTED ON.
THEN DIVISION 4 WILL HAVE MORE FREEDOM TO OPERATE, AND WE CAN SAVE EVEN MORE PEOPLE FROM DEVILS.

LIAR.

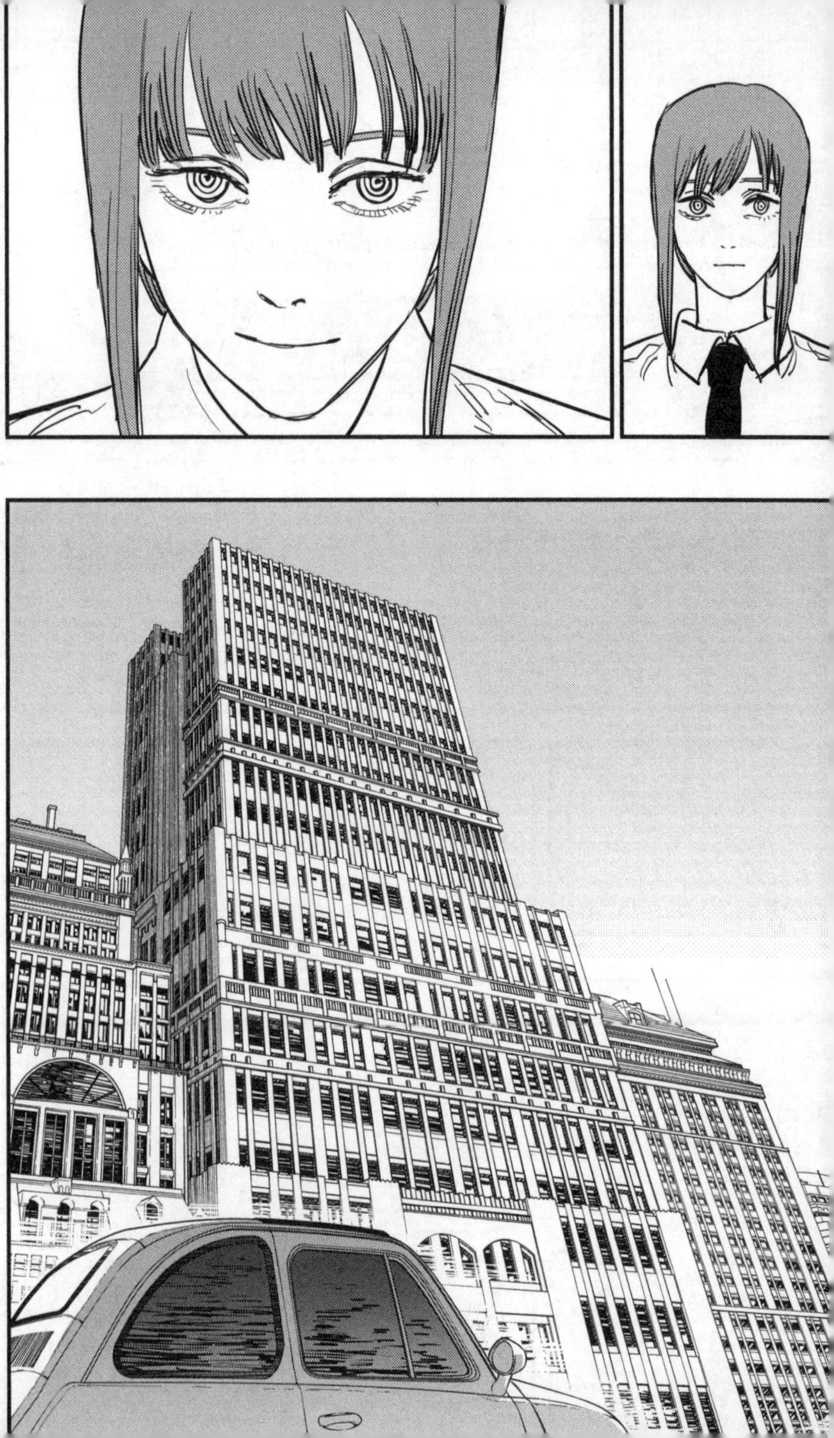

WE'RE HAVING THE BIG BOSS MOVE TO THE VILLA.
YOU SHOULD GO TOO, SIR...
AS LONG AS MAKIMA'S ALIVE, THERE'S NOWHERE IN JAPAN YOU CAN RUN TO.

WE'RE PREPARED TO ENGAGE THE ENEMY RIGHT HERE.
NOW KEEP QUIET.

SHUT UP, GIRL!!
SIR...!

IF GRANDDAD WERE HERE, HE'D NEVER STAND FOR RUNNING AWAY.

PLUS, THAT DAMN DENJI IS IN DIVISION 4...

NEXT TIME, I'LL RIP OUT HIS HEART!

GRAND-
DAD'S
PARTING
GIFT—

A ZOMBIE ARMY MADE OF GOOD-FOR-NOTHINGS WHO COULDN'T PAY BACK THEIR DEBTS.
HUMANS BITTEN BY A ZOMBIE WILL TURN INTO ZOMBIES THEMSELVES.
THAT'S HOW WE'LL FINISH OFF DIVISION 4.

Chain saw man

Chapter 33: Mission Start

Chain saw man

WE'RE GOING TO SIGHTSEE IN TOKYO, THEN RETURN TO KYOTO.

YOU'LL PROBABLY NEVER SEE US AGAIN ANYWAY— SO LET ME ASK YOU SOMETHING, AKI.

WE HEARD YOU'RE AFTER THE GUN DEVIL.
DO YOU REALLY BELIEVE YOU CAN KILL IT?

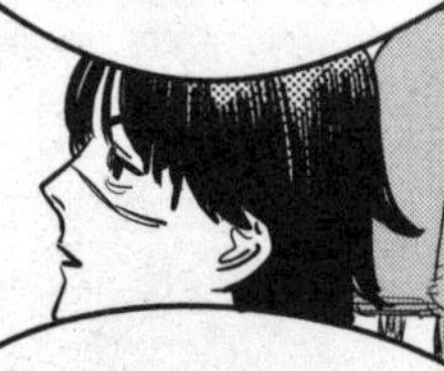
YOU LOST THIS BATTLE TO AN ENEMY WHO KILLED ABOUT 20 SPECIAL DIVISION AGENTS.
WHAT MAKES YOU THINK YOU CAN DEFEAT THE DEVIL THAT KILLED MILLIONS OF PEOPLE AROUND THE WORLD?

SEE, OUR LIVES WERE RUINED BY THE GUN DEVIL TOO. THAT'S WHY WE JOINED PUBLIC SAFETY.

BUT TRYING TO KILL THE GUN DEVIL? WE'D NEVER EVEN CONSIDER IT.
THINKING RATIONALLY, YOU'D KNOW IT'S NOT POSSIBLE.

HONESTLY, WATCHING YOU MAKES ME ANGRY.
YOU'RE SO WEAK. YET YOU GIVE YOURSELF A GOAL LIKE THE MAIN CHARACTER OF A MANGA. IT'S SO CRINGEY IT GIVES ME GOOSEBUMPS.

SEE? I'VE GOT 'EM RIGHT NOW.

DO NOT.

SPARE ME THE COMMENTARY.
ALL YOU NEED TO DO IS STAND BACK AND KEEP YOUR MOUTH SHUT.

WHEN I LOSE AND DIE, THEN YOU'RE WELCOME TO COME AND LAUGH AT ME.

I'M AWARE THAT I'VE STOPPED LOOKING AT MYSELF OBJECTIVELY.
BUT... I ALSO KNOW I COULDN'T GO ON IF I DID.

SLAM

THANK YOU FOR THE ADVICE.

PAFF

AKI!! EVEN THOUGH YOU TICK ME OFF, I'M ROOTING FOR YOU!!
I'LL LEAVE YOU WITH ONE LAST PIECE OF ADVICE!!

EVERY-BODY IN THE SPECIAL DIVISIONS IS INSANE! SO BE CAREFUL!

OUR GUEST IS FROM PUBLIC SAFETY.
BRING OUT THE PRICEY TEA.

THANK YOU VERY MUCH FOR YOUR COOPERATION.

AS I HEAR IT, THE ONE PULLING THE STRINGS IS THIS ***SAWATARI*** GIRL.

OUR YOUNGSTERS WERE APPARENTLY TRICKED INTO MAKING A CONTRACT WITH THE GUN DEVIL, WITH HER BROKERING THE DEAL.

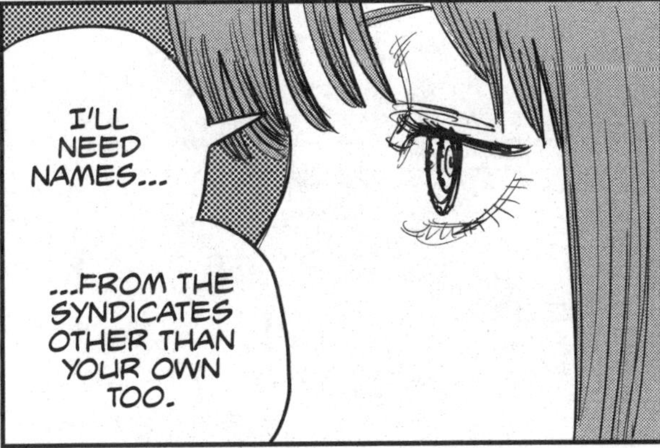

HEY, MISSY...

YOU HAVEN'T GOT A CLUE HOW THIS THING WORKS, DO YA?

EVEN IF I KNEW NAMES, IF IT GOT OUT THAT I SQUEALED, WE'D HAVE AN INTERFAMILY WAR ON OUR HANDS.
RIDICU-LOUS...

IT'S FOR THE SAFETY OF THE PUBLIC.
I'D APPRECIATE YOUR COOPERATION.

MISSY...
ARE YOU FAMILIAR WITH THE PHRASE...
... NECES-SARY EVIL?
F-WOOOOOOOO

SAY WE DESTROYED EACH OTHER. WHAT'D HAPPEN THEN?
FOREIGN MAFIAS WOULD ELBOW THEIR WAY INTO JAPAN THROUGH THE CRACKS, THAT'S WHAT.

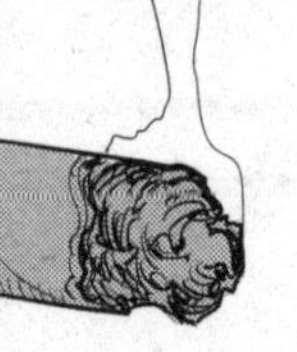
DO WE DO SOME BAD THINGS? SURE.
BUT THE CHINESE MAFIA? THE RUSSIAN MAFIA? THEY COMMIT FAR MORE HORRIBLE DEEDS THAN US.
WE'RE THE ONES HOLDING THEM AT BAY.

JUST LIKE YOU DEVIL HUNTERS KEEP HUMANS SAFE FROM DEVILS...
...WE IN THE YAKUZA KEEP THE JAPANESE PEOPLE SAFE FROM FOREIGNERS.

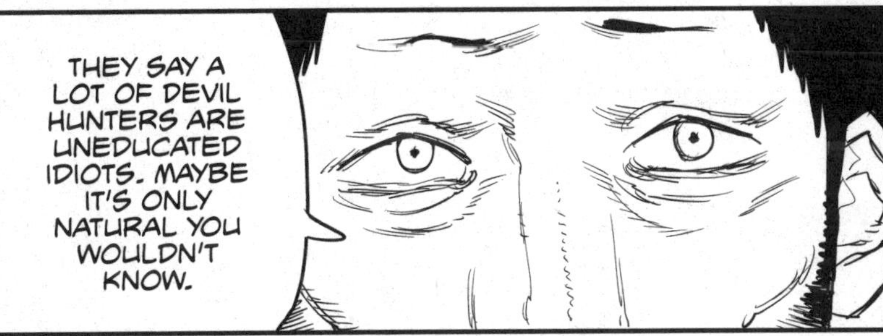
THEY SAY A LOT OF DEVIL HUNTERS ARE UNEDUCATED IDIOTS. MAYBE IT'S ONLY NATURAL YOU WOULDN'T KNOW.

Ha ha ha ha ha ha ha!!

I CAN'T SELL OUT MY OWN FOR CHUMP CHANGE.

THIS ISN'T MONEY.

IT'S EVERY-ONE HERE'S...
... FATHERS' ...
... MOTHERS' ...
... GRAND-MOTHERS' ...
... GRAND-FATHERS' ...

...BROTHERS'...
...SISTERS'...
...LOVERS'...
...AND WIVES'—ALL OF...

...THEIR...
...EYES.

EYES?

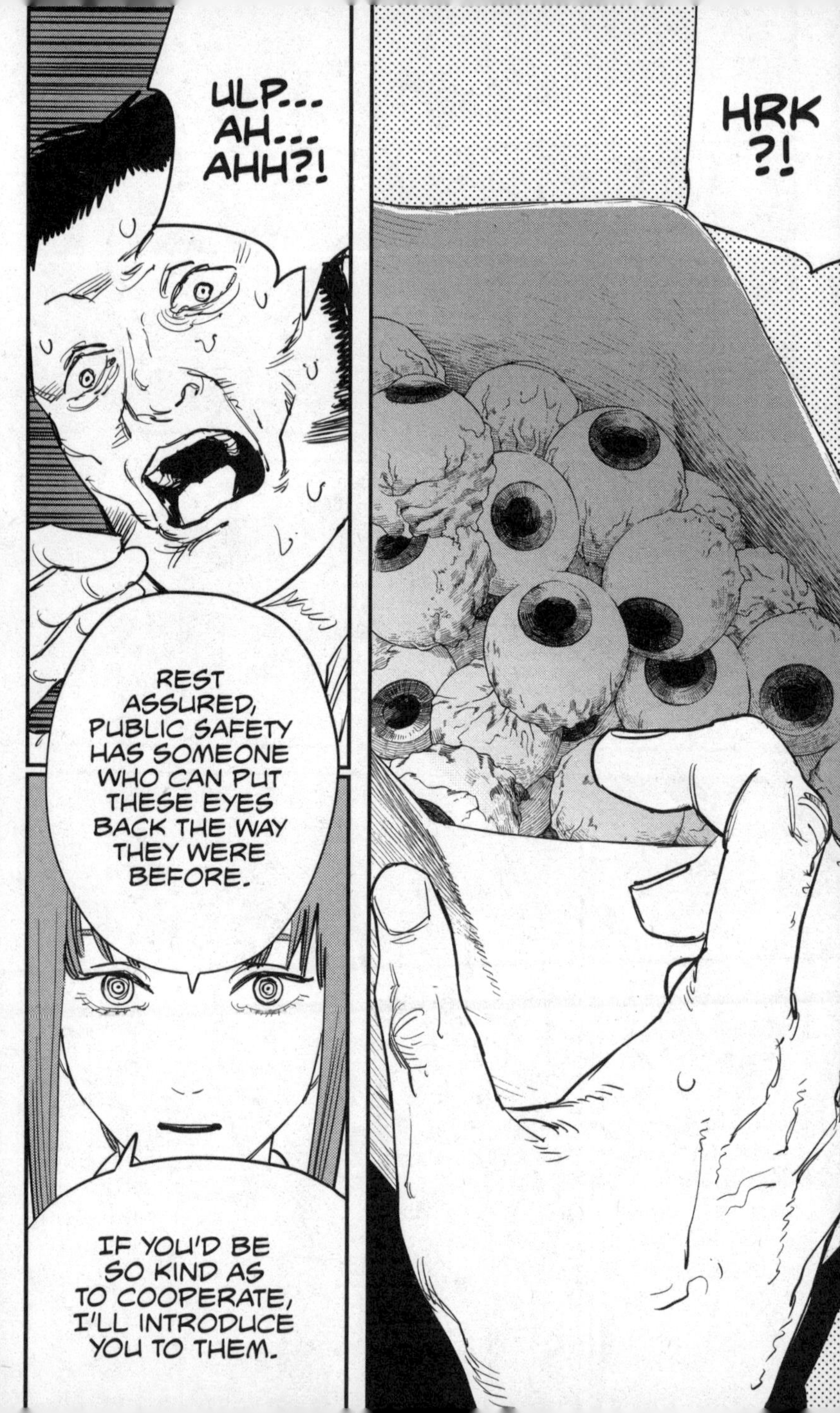
HRK ?!
ULP... AH... AHH?!
REST ASSURED, PUBLIC SAFETY HAS SOMEONE WHO CAN PUT THESE EYES BACK THE WAY THEY WERE BEFORE.
IF YOU'D BE SO KIND AS TO COOPERATE, I'LL INTRODUCE YOU TO THEM.

WHY, YOU ...!!

YOUR NECESSARY EVIL...

...IS JUST AN EXCUSE TO JUSTIFY YOUR OWN CRIMES.

THOSE EXCUSES ARE UNNECES-SARY TO SOCIETY.

THE BASEMENT AND FIRST-FLOOR EXITS ARE SURROUNDED BY DEVIL EXTERMINATION DIVISION 2 AND THE POLICE.
SPECIAL DIVISION 4 IS HANDLING ALL SUPPRESSION EFFORTS INSIDE THE BUILDING.
WE'LL KILL AS MANY PUBLIC SAFETY AGENTS AS POSSIBLE AND TAKE DENJI'S HEART.
AFTERWARD, YOU AND I AT LEAST SHOULD BE ABLE TO ESCAPE IF I USE THE SNAKE.

I'LL
KILL
DENJI.

AHHH
...
UH
?

DON'T
LOSE
YOUR
COOL.

WE'RE THROWING EVERY SINGLE SPECIAL DIVISION AGENT AT THAT BUILDING.

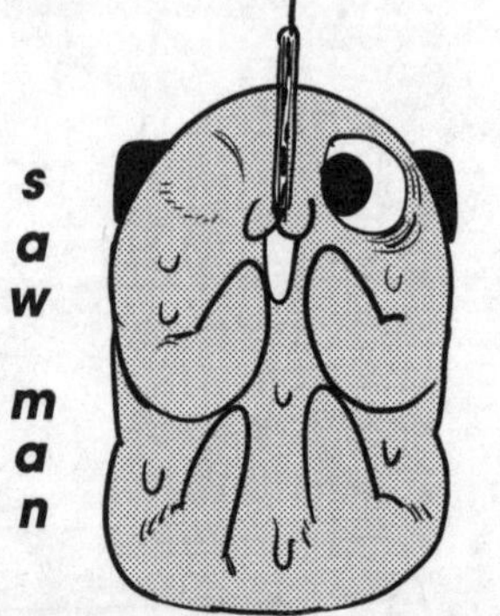
Chain
sawman

Chapter 34: Full Team

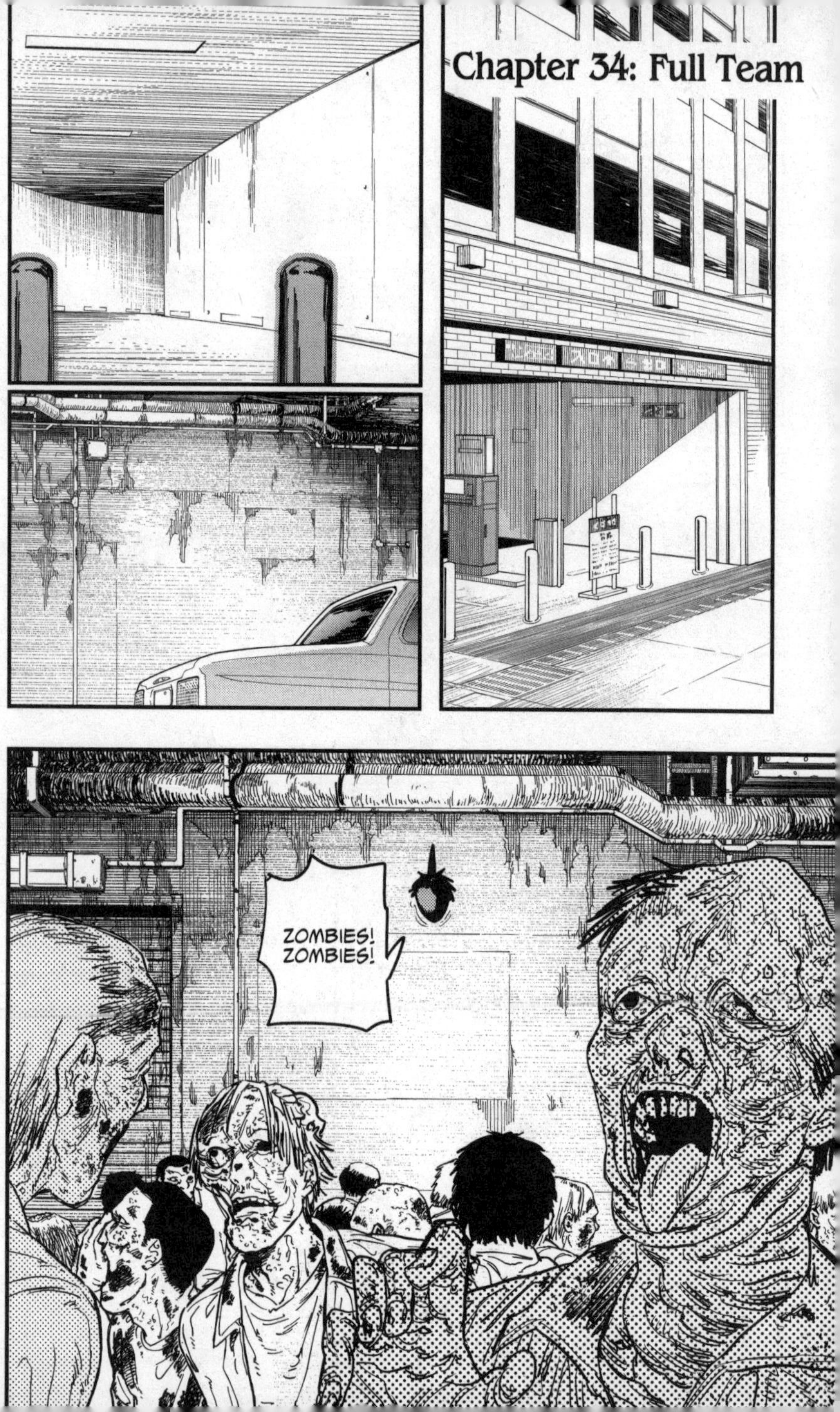

Chapter 34: Full Team

ZOMBIES!
ZOMBIES!

Kya kya kya!
It's all-you-can-eat!!

THE SHARK FIEND.
THIS ONE CAN SWIM IN ANY SURFACE— WALLS, GROUND, YOU NAME IT.
HE CAN ALSO TAKE A DEVIL FORM FOR SHORT PERIODS OF TIME.

FLASH

GWAH!!

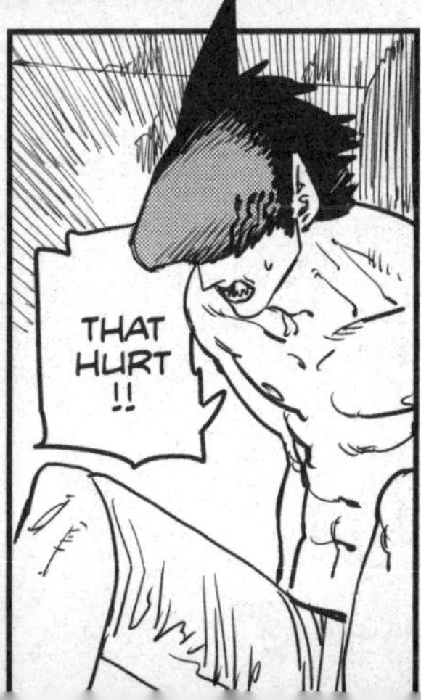
THAT HURT!!

WHOOPS! MY BAD!
SINCE YOU TRIED TO BITE ME, I THOUGHT YOU WERE A ZOMBIE!

THE VIOLENCE FIEND.
UNDER NORMAL CIRCUMSTANCES, WHEN THESE GUYS BECOME FIENDS, THEY'RE WEAKER THAN THEY ARE AS DEVILS...
...BUT THIS ONE IS STILL TOO STRONG EVEN AS A FIEND. SO WE MAKE THE VIOLENCE FIEND WEAR A POISON-DISPENSING MASK.
DO NOT REMOVE THAT MASK UNDER ANY CIRCUM-STANCES.

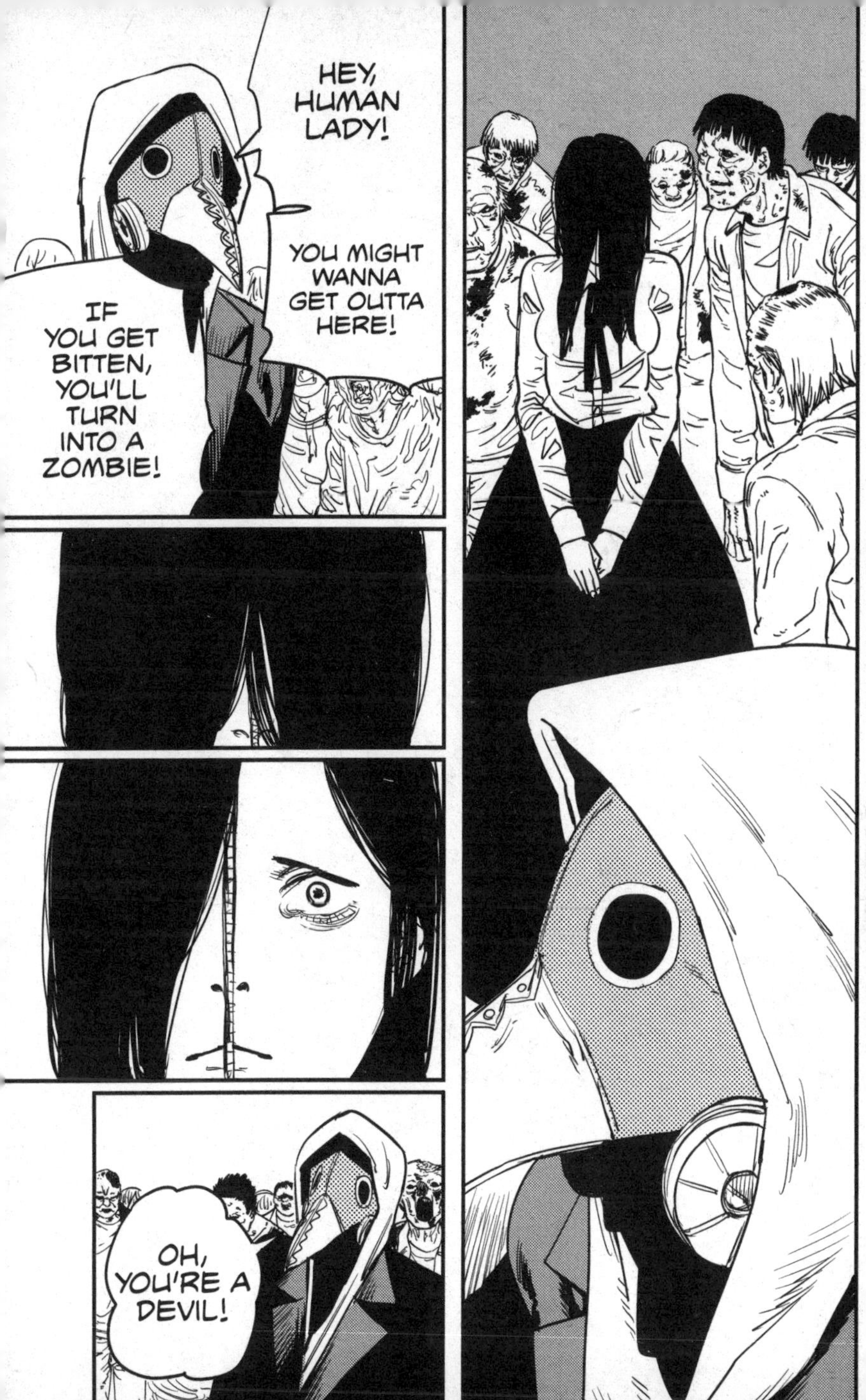
HEY, HUMAN LADY!
YOU MIGHT WANNA GET OUTTA HERE!
IF YOU GET BITTEN, YOU'LL TURN INTO A ZOMBIE!
OH, YOU'RE A DEVIL!

THE SPIDER DEVIL.
SHE USUALLY TAKES A HUMAN SHAPE.
DEVILS WITH HUMANLIKE APPEARANCES TEND TO BE FRIENDLY TO HUMANS, BUT A DEVIL'S A DEVIL.
SHE'LL KILL PEOPLE JUST FOR LOOKING AT HER THE WRONG WAY.

THUD

BLECH... GOT MY SHOES DIRTY...
WHAT A JERK...

THE ANGEL DEVIL.
A UNIQUE CASE— A DEVIL WHO ISN'T HOSTILE TOWARD HUMANS. BUT DO NOT APPROACH.
TOUCH THIS ONE AND YOUR LIFE SPAN WILL BE SIPHONED OFF.

HEY, YOU...
GOT A HANDKER-CHIEF?

I'M SURPRISED YOU'D GET THIS CLOSE TO ME.
IF I TOUCH YOU, I'LL SHORTEN YOUR LIFE SPAN...

IT'S SAFE THROUGH CLOTH, RIGHT?

SHWIP

BANG
BANG
OW. OW.
WHOA!
TSH

THOK

KRAK

DEVIL!
MOVE HIM OUTSIDE.
I'M BEING ORDERED AROUND...
WELL, IT'S BETTER THAN FIGHTING, I GUESS...

消火器

DON'T RESIST. SURRENDER NOW.
SNAKE.
SPIT IT OUT.
HWOO

SON OF A...

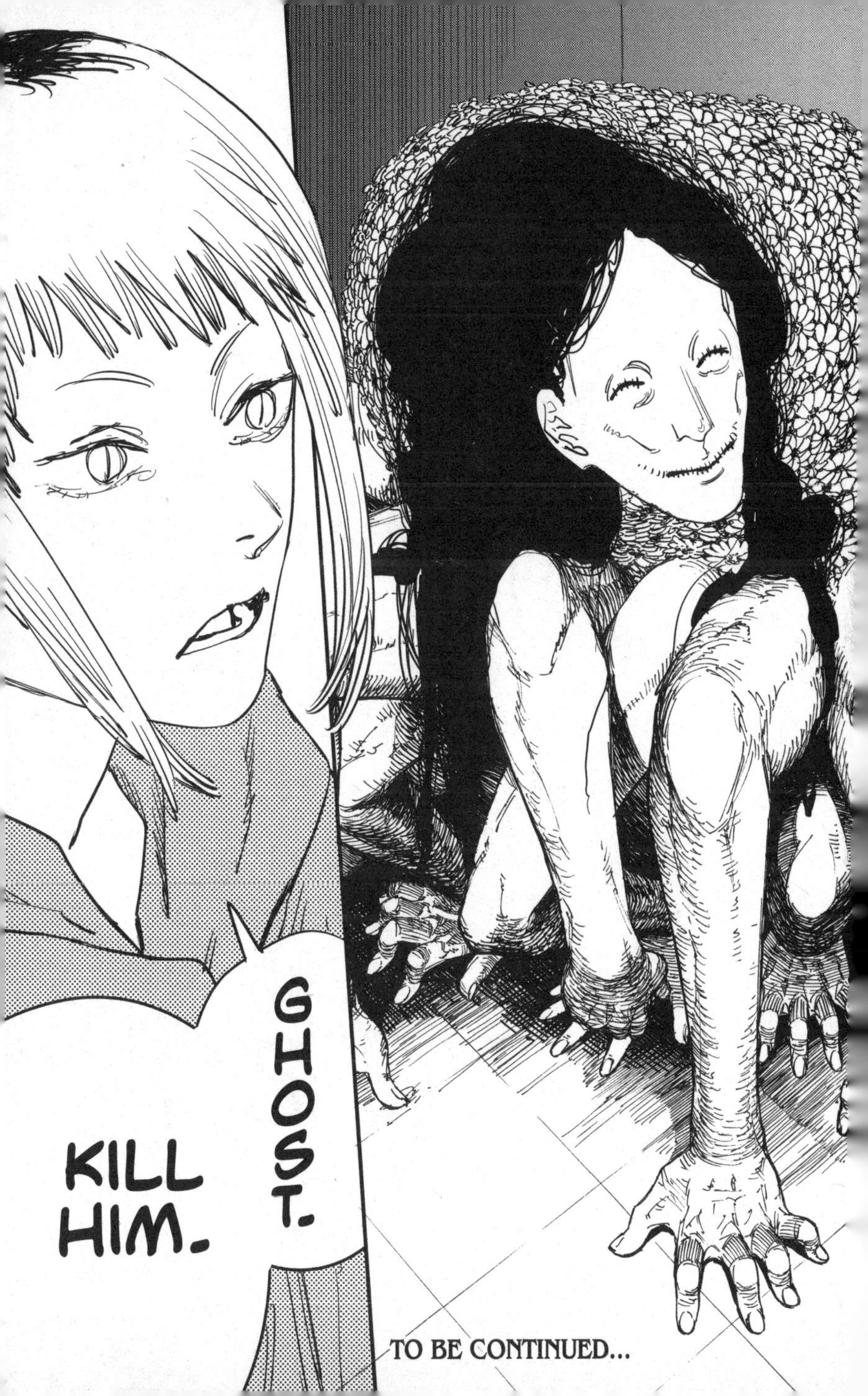
GHOST.
KILL HIM.
TO BE CONTINUED...

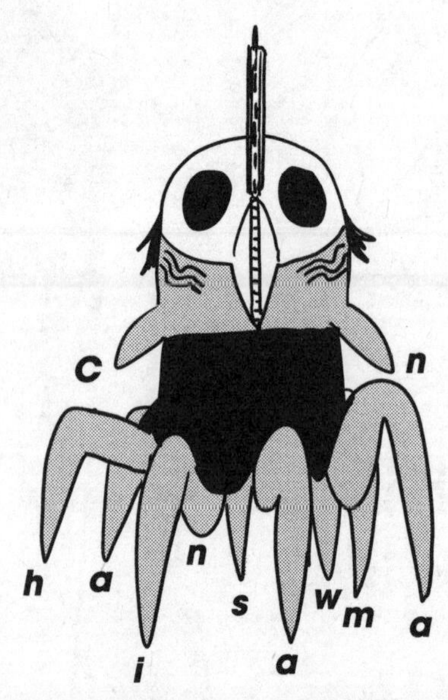
C h a i n s a w m a n

YOU'RE READING THE WRONG WAY!

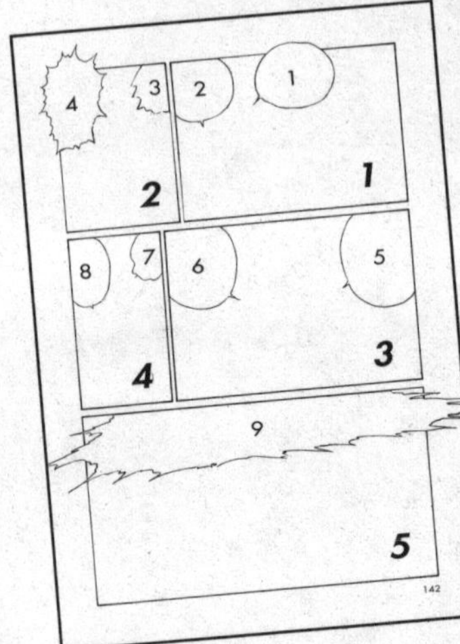

Chainsaw Man reads from right to left, starting in the upper-right corner. Japanese is read from right to left, meaning that action, sound effects and word-balloon order are completely reversed from English order.